Warming Up for

book one

by Cassia Harvey

Edited by Judith Harvey

CHP118
ISBN 978-1-932823-17-2

6403 N. 6th Street
Philadelphia, PA 19126
www.charveypublications.com

Less-advanced (A) pages are structured so that they can be played together with more-advanced (B) pages.

Contents

Warmups in G major

Daily Exercise (A)

Cassia Harvey

March (A)

L. Mozart, arr. Harvey

3

4

Daily Exercise (B)

March (B)

L. Mozart, arr. Harvey

5

Finger Workout (A)

Sonata (A)

Cimarosa, arr. Harvey

Warming Up for Violin, Book One

Finger Workout (B)

Sonata (B)

Cimarosa, arr. Harvey

Finger Twister (A)

Dill Pickle Rag (A)

Johnson, arr. Harvey

Finger Twister (B)

Dill Pickle Rag (B)

Johnson, arr. Harvey

Warmups in D major

Daily Exercise (A)

Variations on a Theme (A)

Romberg, arr. Harvey

15

Daily Exercise (B)

Variations on a Theme (B)

Romberg, arr. Harvey

Finger Workout (A)

Rondo (A)

Mozart, arr. Harvey

Warming Up for Violin, Book One

Finger Workout (B)

Rondo (B)

Mozart, arr. Harvey

Warming Up for Violin, Book One

Finger Twister (A)

Miss Ratray's Reel (A)

Trad., arr. Harvey

Finger Twister (B)

Miss Ratray's Reel (B)

Trad., arr. Harvey

Warmups in C major

Daily Exercise (A)

Mason's Apron (A)

Trad., arr. Harvey

Warming Up for Violin, Book One

Daily Exercise (B)

Mason's Apron (B)

Trad., arr. Harvey

Finger Workout (A)

Bourree (A)

Bach, arr. Harvey

Finger Workout (B)

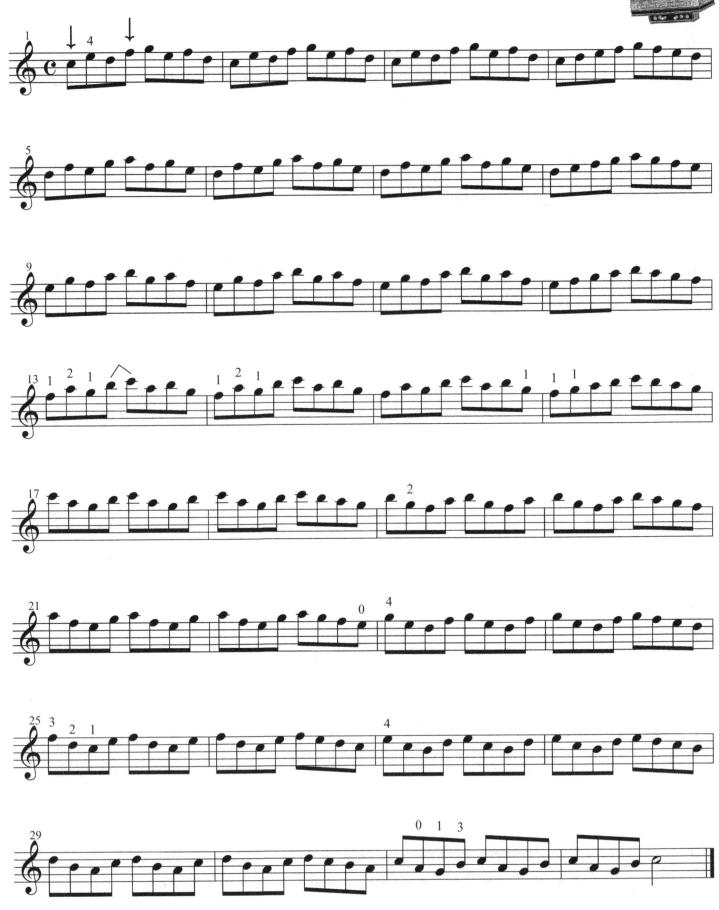

Bourree (B)

Bach, arr. Harvey

Warming Up for Violin, Book One

Finger Twister (A)

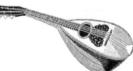

Grazioso (A)

Cimarosa, arr. Harvey

Finger Twister (B)

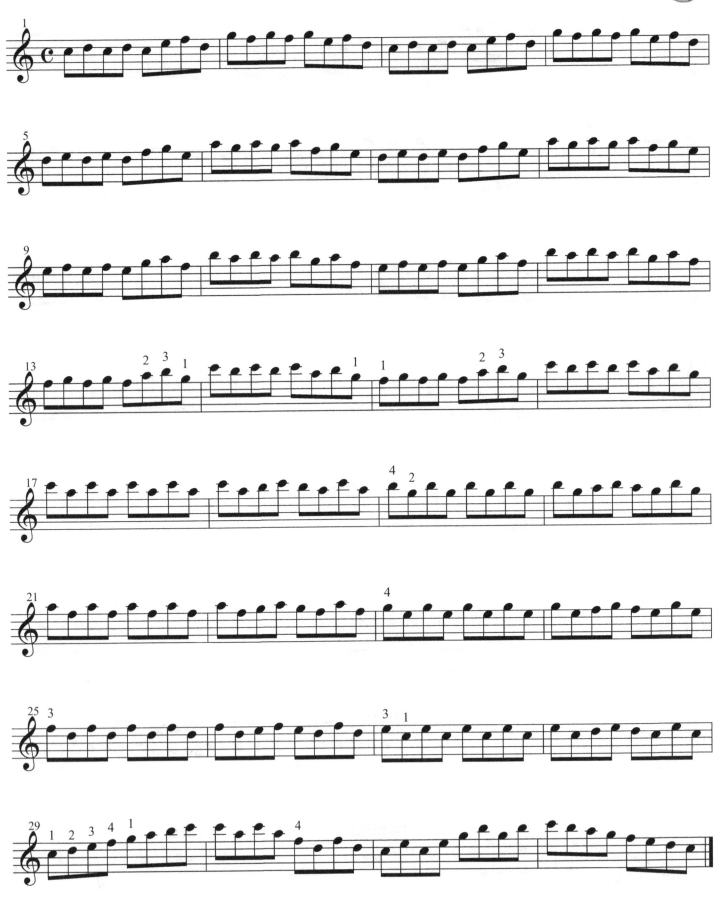

Grazioso (B)

Cimarosa, arr. Harvey

Warmups in F major

Daily Exercise (A)

Variation (A)

Paganini, arr. Harvey

Warming Up for Violin, Book One

Daily Exercise (B)

Variation (B)

Paganini, arr. Harvey

Finger Workout (A)

Allegro (A)

Paxton, arr. Harvey

Finger Workout (B)

Allegro (B)

Paxton, arr. Harvey

46

Finger Twister (A)

The Dashing Sergeant (A)

Trad., arr. Harvey

Warming Up for Violin, Book One

Finger Twister (B)

The Dashing Sergeant (B)

Trad., arr. Harvey

Warming Up for Violin, Book One

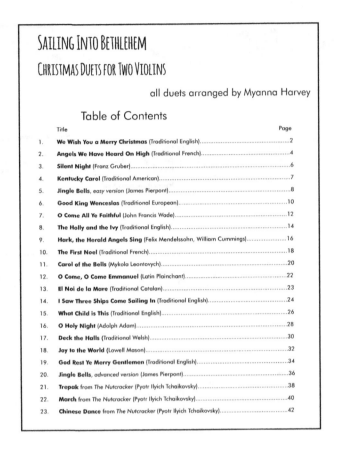

SAILING INTO BETHLEHEM

CHRISTMAS DUETS FOR TWO VIOLINS

all duets arranged by Myanna Harvey

Table of Contents

CHP333

CHP334

CHP335

Made in the USA
Middletown, DE
25 August 2024

59653907R00031